Creating and Consuming Media Messages with Purpose

A Guide for Educators

Jennifer W. Shewmaker, Ph.D. and Amy Boone, M.Ed.

Edited by: Lindsey D. Reinert, Ed.D.
Interior design: The Printed Page
Cover design: Kelly Crimi

Published by
Gifted Unlimited, LLC
12340 U.S. Highway 42, No. 453
Goshen, KY 40026
www.giftedunlimitedllc.com

© 2021 by Jennifer W. Shewmaker, Ph.D. and Amy Boone, M.Ed.

ISBN: 978-1-953360-02-1

All rights reserved under International and Pan-American Copyright Conventions. Unless otherwise noted, no part of this book may be reproduced, stored in a retrieval system, or transmitted in any form or by any means—electronic, mechanical, photocopying, or otherwise—without express written permission of the publisher, except for brief quotations or critical reviews.

Printed and bound in the United States of America using partially recycled paper.

Gifted Unlimited and associated logos are trademarks and/or registered trademarks of Gifted Unlimited.

At the time of this book's publication, all facts and figures cited are the most current available. All telephone numbers, addresses, and website URLs are accurate and active; all publications, organizations, websites, and other resources exist as described in this book; and all have been verified as of the time this book went to press. The author(s) and Gifted Unlimited make no warranty or guarantee concerning the information and materials given out by organizations or content found at websites, and we are not responsible for any changes that occur after this book's publication. If you find an error or believe that a resource listed here is not as described, please contact Gifted Unlimited.

Acknowledgents

We would like to thank the Adams Center for Teaching and Learning for creating a space to explore ideas and create new opportunities for learning and our colleagues at Abilene Christian University for joining us in our adventures in learning. Thank you to Dr. Mary Christopher for her leadership in the field of Gifted Education and in the Hardin Simmons University Threshold Camp. We would also like to thank our families for their support and their belief in the importance of our pursuits.

Contents

Introduction — 1
   References — 4
   Vocabulary: — 6

Media Intent and Audience — 7
   Reference — 8
   Bloom's level of thinking: analysis — 8
   Extension: Bloom's level of thinking: justification and evaluation — 10

Identity — 11
   References — 12
   Bloom's level of thinking: evaluation — 13
   Extension: Bloom's level of thinking: evaluation — 14

Implicit Bias — 16
   References — 17
   Bloom's level of thinking: analysis — 17
   Extension: Bloom's level of thinking: application, evaluation — 18

Bias and Worldview — 20
   References — 21
   Bloom's level of thinking: evaluation — 21
   Extension: Bloom's level of thinking: evaluation — 22

Stereotypes and Halo Effect — 24
   References — 25
   Bloom's level of thinking: evaluation — 26
   Extension: Bloom's level of thinking: application and analysis — 27

Permanence of Generating online content — 28
   References — 29
   Bloom's level of thinking: analysis — 29
   Extension: Bloom's level of thinking: application and evaluation — 31

Being an Active Consumer — 32
   References — 33
   Bloom's level of thinking: evaluation — 34
   Extension: Bloom's level of thinking: evaluation — 35

Celebrity Culture — 37
   Resources — 38
   Bloom's level of thinking: Evaluation — 38
   Extension: Bloom's level of thinking: evaluation — 39

Data Literacy: What is Big Data and why is it important for us to understand? — 41
   References — 42
   Bloom's level of thinking: synthesis, evaluation — 43
   Extension: Bloom's level of thinking: evaluation — 44
   Student personal information form — 46

Media Creation — 47
   Bloom's level of thinking: evaluation — 48
   Extension: Bloom's level of thinking: application and evaluation — 49

Creating and Consuming Media Messages with Purpose: A Guide for Educators

Teens and tweens are both involved with and influenced by the media. The images and narratives that they absorb from the media shape the way that they see the world. Media provides a lens through which our students see how the world is supposed to work; what makes someone valuable, what is important in life, what is expected of them in society. Children and adolescents today have become media consumers to a degree that was not possible in the past. With the advent of mobile technology, they have access to media that is unparalleled in any other time in our history.

All forms of media have been identified as important socializing forces that deliver messages to children and adolescents about identity (ter Bogt, Engels, Bogers, 2010). To understand the effects of media on our students' development, the bioecological theory is a useful model demonstrating how environmental factors can affect a developing person's response to media. This model, developed by Urie Bronfenbrenner (1979; 1992, 2005; Bronfenbrenner & Morris, 1998; 2006) contends that both a person's temperament and the setting in which she lives lead one to learn, think, and grow in particular ways. Bronfenbrenner conceptualizes a developing person's setting as being made up of several interacting systems. These include the microsystem, which is made up of those closest to and most involved with the individual, such as the family, friends, school, and close community. The exosystem is made up of those systems that are further removed but with which the person or those in their microsystem, such as parents, tend to interact regularly. This includes the mass media, the parent's work environment, and so forth. Lastly, the macrosystem is the larger system in which the individual functions, and includes things like the culture, federal laws and systems and so on. There are four components within this model that are crucial to child and adolescent development. These are:

- Process
- Person
- Context
- Time

(PPCT; Bronfenbrenner, 2005, Bronfenbrenner & Morris, 2006)

The idea is that to understand child development, we need to consider each of these four components. For example, each individual develops through the **process** of interacting with those within the immediate environment, including those close relationships, such as family and peers. A person's development is also influenced through interactions that she has with things within the wider (or macro) environment, such as media and marketing. At the same time, we need to be aware that elements of the **person** her or himself, such as temperament and past experience, will influence the individual's interpretations, experiences of and responses to their interactions with these different systems. The **context** of the systems of influence (micro, exo and macro) shapes the child's understanding of and ability to respond to interactions with media and marketing. The **time** in which he is growing and learning influence the type of environment that the child will engage with as they develop (Shewmaker, 2015).

The time in which our students are growing up is particularly important. Both Mark Prensky (2001a, 2001b, 2012) and, more recently, Jean Twenge (2017) note that the development and ubiquity of access to digital technology has resulted in a significant shift in the way that people communicate. Prensky termed today's students "digital natives," meaning that they are "native speakers of the digital language of computers, video games and the Internet" (Prensky, 2001a, pg. 1). Similarly, Jean Twenge (2017) has labeled those born between 1995 and 2012 as "iGen", with a focus on the way that the ubiquity of smartphones and social media have shaped this age group. As we think about aiding our students in building skills to critique and create media, we need to understand that their digital native or iGen status may mean that they understand and approach media differently than those of us who did not grow up during this time of easy access to digital technology and social media. However, it is also important to keep in mind that there is an economic digital divide amongst this generation, with some students having ready and frequent access to mobile digital technology while others do not. This means that your students may have different levels of digital literacy and varying frequency of use of digital technologies (Sorgo, Bartol, Donicar & Both Podgornik, 2017).

Bronfenbrenner viewed the process of development as one in which the child can learn to fit into the existing environment and expectations, but can also change the order of things through their own actions (Tudge, Mokrova, Hatfield, & Karnik, 2009). When we provide students with the tools to critique and challenge the messages from media and marketing, they can become change makers. Their actions through media literacy programs, activism, and creation can lead to change in their environment. As digital natives or members of iGen, they can use their unique perspective to not only use media, but to shape it.

Adolescents are in the process of constructing their identity, and the media is one of the influences in their lives that they use to help them figure out who they are, who they want to be, and who they think they should be. Adolescents are active media users, making sense of what they see and hear from their own individual perspective and experience. Developmental research has clearly demonstrated that until the age of eight, children cannot separate persuasive messages from entertainment. Even pre-teens and those in their early teens are at a disadvantage in identifying advertisements when they are presented online rather than in television or print (An, Jin, & Park, 2014; Rozendaal, Buijzen, & Valkenburg, 2011; Soontae & Stern, 2011; Mallinckrodt & Mizerski, 2007; Gunter, Oates & Blades, 2005; Oates, Blades, & Gunter, 2002). These facts make it more important than ever for adults to pay attention to the media that children and adolescents consume and to consider how our students can become active, critical media consumers.

Research indicates that children spend a lot of time with media. Specifically, children spend an average of 5 hours on electronic devices per day (Crouch, 2016). Recent research has noted that 42% of children ages 0-8 now have their own tablet and 98% of children aged 0-18 years live in a home with a television and a mobile device. Forty seven percent of tweens and 57% of teens reported having a television in their room. Forty two percent of children aged 0 to 8, 34% aged 8 to 12 and 37% aged 13-18 live in houses where the TV is on "always" or "most of the time." Total screen media time each day for children aged 0-8 was reported as 2 hours and 19 minutes. For 8-12 year olds reported being exposed to media an average of 5:55 hours a day and 13-18 year olds reported media usage at 8 hours and 56 minutes each day (Rideout, 2015; 2017). When we consider entertainment screen media, 8-12 year olds spend an average of 4:44 hours a day while teens spend 7:22, not including time spent for school or homework (Rideout & Robb, 2019). The biggest change in recent years has been the increase in video viewing, with the number of young people reporting that they watch videos everyday doubling since 2015. Adolescents also report that the time they spend watching videos has doubled since 2015, increasing from half an hour to an hour per day (Rideout & Robb, 2019).

The development of mobile technology means that students are more highly involved with media than ever before due to increased accessibility. This accessibility makes media messages even more powerful and is a key issue when considering the way that students use media today. Mobile devices that access media, such as the iPhone, Android, and iPad, have made media readily accessible to an ever increasing number of young people. The past five years has seen an increase in the ownership of mobile devices among eight to eighteen year olds. Ninety eight percent of the homes of children surveyed reported having a mobile device and 45% of children, 77% of tweens and 100% of teens surveyed own their own mobile device, either a tablet or a smartphone. Smartphones have morphed from a vehicle for communication to a way to connect with media. Young people who own a cell phone tend to use it more often to play or watch media than they do for talking to another person (Rideout, 2015; 2017). Interestingly, in recent years we have seen an increase in the use of mobile devices to connect with others via social media. Fifty-eight percent of teens use social media, spending an average of two hours each day on it. This tends to be an activity that increases with age, with only 15% of 8-12 year olds reporting the regular use of social media while 58% of teens report its use (Rideout & Robb, 2019; Rideout, 2015).

This increase in media exposure and use of media to share about one's self has made it vitally important for those working with children and adolescents to understand how media affects their development and to identify strategies that can create critical, empowered media consumers and makers. It's important for us to remember that media is a tool that can be used to promote both positive and negative messages to our students and allow our students to share their own perspectives through media creation. While some media can lead to negative outcomes, media messages that challenge stereotypes and promote complex views of people can open up avenues for great conversations. This book has been created to help teachers provide opportunities for their students to begin to create and consume media messages with purpose, empowering them to be active consumers and creators. The book is broken into separate sessions that focus on different aspects of media literacy. Each session provides the teacher with a brief literature review, Core Social Emotional Learning Competencies related to CASEL, a lesson plan and extension suggestions. You can find a deeper look into the research and an extension of the themes discussed in this book, with a focus on sexualized media, in the book *Sexualized media messages and our children: Teaching kids to be smart critics and consumers* by Dr. Jennifer W. Shewmaker.

References

An, S., Jin, H. S., & Park, E. H. (2014). Children's Advertising Literacy for Advergames: Perception of the Game as Advertising. *Journal of Advertising*, *43*(1), 63-72. doi:10.1080/00913367.2013.795123

Bogt, T. t., Engels, R., Bogers, S., & Kloosterman, M. (2010). 'Shake It Baby, Shake It': Media Preferences, Sexual Attitudes and Gender Stereotypes Among Adolescents. *Sex Roles*, *63*(11-12), 844-859. doi:10.1007/s11199-010-9815-1

Bronfenbrenner, U. (1979). *The Ecology of Human Development* (Cambridge, MA: Harvard University Press, 1979)

Bronfenbrenner, U. (1992). *Six Theories of Child Development: Revised Formulations and Current Issues*, ed. Ross Vasta (London: Jessica Kingsley) 187-249.

Bronfenbrenner, U. (2005). *Making Human Beings Human* (Thousand Oaks, CA: Sage).

Bronfenbrenner, U. & Morris, P. A. (1998). "The Ecology of Developmental Processes," in *Theoretical Models of Human Development*, ed. Richard M. Lerner, vol. 1 of *Handbook of Child Psychology*, 5th ed., ed. William Damon (New York: Wiley, 1998), 993-1028;

Bronfenbrenner, U. & Morris, P. A. (2006). "The Bioecological Model of Human Development," in *Theoretical Models of Human Development*, ed. Richard M. Lerner, vol. 1 of *Handbook of Child Psychology*, 5th ed., ed. William Damon (New York: Wiley).

Crouch, A. (2017). *The tech-wise family : everyday steps for putting technology in its proper place*. Grand Rapids : Baker Books, [2017].

Evans, C. & Robertson, W. (2020). The four phases of the digital natives debate. *Human Behavior and Emerging Technologies*, 2, 269-277. https://doi.org/10.1002/hbe2.196

Gunter, B., Oates, C., & Blades, M. (2005). *Advertising to Children on TV: Content, Impact, and Regulation*. Mahwah, N.J.: Routledge.

Mallinckrodt, V., & Mizerski, D. (2007). The effects of playing an advergame on young children's perceptions, preferences, and requests. *Journal of Advertising*, *36*(2), 87-100.

Oates, C., Blades, M., & Gunter, B. (2002). Children and television advertising: When do they understand persuasive intent?. *Journal of Consumer Behaviour*, *1*(3), 238.

Prensky, M. (2012). From digital natives to digital wisdom : hopeful essays for 21st century learning. Corwin.

Prensky, M. (2001a). Digital Natives, Digital Immigrants Part 1. On the Horizon, 9(5), 1.

Prensky, M. (2001b). Digital Natives, Digital Immigrants Part 2: Do They Really Think Differently? On the Horizon, 9(6), 1.

Rideout, V., and Robb, M. B. (2019). *The Common Sense census: Media use by tweens and teens, 2019*. San Francisco, CA: Common Sense Media.

Rideout, V. (2017). The Common Sense census: Media use by kids age zero to eight. San Francisco, CA: Common Sense Media.

Rideout, V. (2015). The Common Sense census: Media use by tweens and teens. San Francisco, CA: Common Sense Media.

Rozendaal, E., Buijzen, M. and Valkenburg, P. (2011), "Children's understanding of advertiser's persuasive tactics," *International Journal of Advertising*, 30 (2), 329–50.

Shewmaker, J. W. (2015). Sexualized media messages and out children: Teaching kids to be smart critics and consumers. Santa Barbara, CA: Praeger.

Soontae, A., & Stern, S. (2011). Mitigating the effects of advergames on children. *Journal of Advertising, 40*(1), 43-56.

Šorgo, A., Bartol, T., Dolničar, D., & Boh Podgornik, B. (2017). Attributes of digital natives as predictors of information literacy in higher education: Digital natives and information literacy. *British Journal of Educational Technology, 48*(3), 749–767. https://doi.org/10.1111/bjet.12451

Tudge, J. H., Mokrova, I., Hatfield, B. E., & Karnik, R. B. (2009). Uses and misuses of Bronfenbrenner's bioecological theory of human development. *Journal of Family Theory & Review, 1*(4), 198-210. doi:10.1111/j.1756-2589.2009.00026.x

Twenge, J. M. (2017). Have smartphones destroyed a generation? *The Atlantic*, 20 (September 2017), https://www.theatlantic.com/magazine/archive/2017/0a9/has-the-smartphone-destroyed-a-generation/534198/.

Vocabulary:

- **Producer**: one who creates, makes
- **Consumer**: one who uses, spends, consumes
- **Online disinhibition**: lack of restraint one feels when communicating **online** in comparison to communicating in-person
- **Unconscious bias**: social stereotypes about certain groups of people that individuals form outside their own conscious awareness
- **Bias**: a disproportionate weight in favor of or against an idea or thing, usually in a way that is closed-minded, prejudicial, or unfair
- **Worldview**: the lens through which we view the world, the assumptions that we make about truth, value, and humanity
- **Stereotypes**: a widely held but fixed and oversimplified image or idea of a particular type of person or thing.
- **Halo effect**: the tendency for positive impressions of a person, company, brand or product in one area to positively influence one's opinion or feelings in other areas
- **Fake news**: untrue information presented as news
- **Clickbait**: content (often headlines) whose main purpose is to attract attention and encourage visitors to click on a link to a particular web page
- **Propaganda**: information, especially of a biased or misleading nature, used to promote or publicize a particular political cause or point of view
- **Parody**: a composition that imitates the style of another composition, normally for comic effect and often by applying that style to an outlandish or inappropriate subject
- **Big data**: data that contains greater variety arriving in increasing volumes and with ever-higher velocity
- **Big tech**: the largest and most dominant companies in the information technology industry of the United States, especially Amazon, Apple, Alphabet, Facebook and Microsoft
- **Ethos**: credibility, how credible the audience/reader perceives the writer or speaker to be
- **Pathos**: emotional connection, how are feelings engaged
- **Logos**: facts, logic

Media Intent and Audience

Session one: This session will focus on media's intent and audience. When a person encounters a media message, they must ask where the message originated. They should also consider who is the target audience of the media message. The activities for this session include identifying types of language used in media messages and how a media message captures the attention of the consumer.

Core SEL Competency: Social awareness

In this session, we will investigate how students can become empowered to critique media, with a focus on identifying the intent of the media creator and the intended audience. What is media, after all, but the creation of something that shares an individual or group's worldview with others? When students begin to understand that each piece of media or marketing that they consume has been crafted to promote a particular perspective, they can learn to identify that perspective and ask themselves how they feel about it. Do they agree or disagree with the worldview presented? We will focus on ways to give students the ability to become aware of what they are consuming, identify the worldview being presented, and decide what they think of it.

It is a good thing to be critically aware of the meanings and implications of the media and platforms with which we interact. The recognition that a piece of media may be sending messages that do not align with one's core values is the first step to becoming a critical media consumer. For students who are digital natives/iGen, digital media may have been a part of their life for as long as they can remember. Sometimes that kind of familiarity makes it difficult for students to identify the underlying messages, but you may find that other students naturally make assumptions that everything they consume has been designed to sell something or influence them in some way. This variety of perspectives means that it is vital for teachers to take the time to use specific strategies to begin to build digital literacy for all students.

Some of these strategies have been adapted from ideas presented in the work of Renee Hobbs (2011), a media literacy expert. Her book *Digital and Media Literacy: Connecting Culture and Classroom* provides an excellent guide to understanding the importance of digital and media literacy along with information and specific plans for using literacy activities in the classroom with varied curriculum.

The first step is to ask a few questions about the target audience:

○ Who does this message come from?

○ Who is the target audience according to the developer?

○ Paying attention to what you see and hear, who seems to be the target audience to you?

Next we want to help our students consider the messages that are being shared through the piece of media. As we explore this issue, we can ask questions such as, what message is clearly displayed through words, music, images and stories? What about the unspoken messages? Are there impressions that you get very clearly whether they are or are not spoken?

Lastly, we will help students consider the values that are being shared through a piece of media. It's important that students know that each piece of media that they consume is representing some sort of value, and to learn to ask themselves what those values are, how they compare to the student's own value system, and how they feel about those being represented through that piece of media. We'll guide our students through considering this by asking them to consider, what values are presented? What positive and negative messages come through? How do these compare to your own value system?

Reference

Renee Hobbs. *Digital and Media Literacy: Connecting Culture and Classroom.* (Thousand Oaks, California : Corwin Press, 2011). 232.

Bloom's level of thinking: analysis

Objective: In their study of media sources, students will compare various media and determine each type's intent/audience.

Grouping: whole class and smaller groups

Materials and resources: copies of the local newspaper, copies of another large newspaper in your state, access via the classroom computer and cell phones to twitter and other appropriate social media sites

Time: 30-45 minutes

Description of the learning process:

The teacher will:

1. Randomly pass out copies of the local newspapers to students (about one for every three students to share). Ask students to identify 2-3 main NON-LOCAL stories they notice (could be state, but preferably national or global).

2. Invite students to write a summary phrase of the stories on the whiteboard and if someone has already written the one they found, make a tally mark beside it.

3. Lead students in selecting 2-3 stories that seem to be the most prevalent.

4. Identify a few students who have internet access on their phones and/or who could use a classroom computer to access social media of some sort.

5. Divide the class into four groups: group 1 takes all the local papers, group 2 takes the other newspapers, group 3 will have their phones on social media (If you are working with early middle school students, you may need to intentionally group students together who have access to social media since many of them may not have social media accounts yet), group 4 will have their phones searching on google FOR THOSE SPECIFIC STORIES from other sites such as TV news stories (monitor the phone groups closely!!!).

6. For 5-6 minutes only, ask students to identify how the writer captures attention with the title and the initial sentence(s) FOR THE CHOSEN STORIES USING ONLY THEIR GROUP'S MEDIA… local newspaper, other state newspaper, social media, or other source.

7. Ask students to identify what kind of language is used? Is it formal? Highly educated? Casual? Does it try to lure you into reading? How?

8. Gather students back into the large group and ask for volunteers to describe what the group found in the articles/sources.

9. Lead students in making conclusions about what various media sources are appealing to and who their audiences might be. Also, lead them in identifying how they can determine what to expect when turning to the various news sources for important information and why this is important.

10. As time permits, lead students in writing a headline that would be for twitter (140 characters) or the local newspaper or the other state newspaper or a TV news outlet for a different story to see if they can differentiate how different media attracts its readers/viewers.

The student will:

1. In groups of three, identify 2-3 main NON-LOCAL stories (could be state, but preferably national or global).

2. Write a summary phrase of the stories on the whiteboard and if someone has already written the one your group found, make a tally mark beside it.

3. Select 2-3 stories that seem to be the most prevalent.

4. Once the class is divided into four groups: group 1 takes all the local papers, group 2 takes the other newspapers, group 3 will have their phones on social media, group 4 will have phones searching on google FOR THOSE SPECIFIC STORIES from other sites such as TV news stories.

5. For 5-6 minutes only, identify how the writer captures your attention with the title and the initial sentence(s) FOR THE CHOSEN STORIES USING ONLY YOUR GROUP'S MEDIA… local newspaper, other state newspaper, social media, or other source.

6. Answer the following questions: What kind of language is used? Is it formal? Highly educated? Casual? Does it try to lure you into reading? How?

7. Gather back into the large group. One group member will describe what the group found in the articles/sources.

8. Draw conclusions about what various media sources are appealing to and who their audiences might be. Identify how you can determine what to expect when turning to various news sources for important information and why this is important.

9. As time permits, write a headline that would be for twitter (140 characters) or the local newspaper or the other state newspaper or a TV news outlet for a different story.

Extension:
Bloom's level of thinking: justification and evaluation

Grouping: whole class and individual or pairs

Materials: access to computer or iPad

Time: 45 minutes-one hour

Students are now more aware of various media sources and have identified their intent/audience. As a class, think of a current newsworthy person or situation that various media outlets might represent differently based on their intent or audience. Using the prior knowledge from the lesson, students will create a news piece (print, audio, or video) from one specific perspective. Students will need to consider the title, word choice, emphasis, tone, and their audience's education level/expectation. Students will create their piece without sharing their unique perspective. As the students share their products, the other students will test their ability to discern the intent and audience of the presenter by determining the presenter's perspective. Share as a group how the students drew conclusions about the intent and audience.

Identity

Session two: This session will focus on identity. In their study of interaction with media, students will explore connections between identity in real life and identity online.

SEL Core Competency: Self-awareness

In this session students will have the opportunity to consider how they and others use social media to represent themselves. They will explore the idea that identity online is chosen and curated, with varying degrees of connection to face-to-face identity.

Children and adolescents are in the process of constructing their identity, and media is one of the influences in their lives that guides them in that process. It's been suggested that media influence development in adolescents in areas such as building social connections as well as forming identity (Twenge, Martin & Spitzberg, 2019). Research has found that adolescents report increasing use of social media (Twenge et al. 2019, Rideout & Robb, 2019). As Twenge has noted of iGen, or what Prensky would call digital natives, the combination of increasing use of social media and access to smartphones means that social media and texting have replaced traditional social activities for many (Twenge, 2017).

In a 2018 national survey, 81% of teenagers reported using social media, with 70% of those teens reporting that they use it more than once a day, 38% saying they use it multiple times an hour and 16% "almost constantly" (Rideout & Robb, 2018). More recent surveys have shown that teens continue to spend about 1:10 on social media a day, but more are reporting using it everyday, up to 63% in 2019 from 45% in 2015 (Rideout & Robb, 2019).

The availability of mobile devices with cameras and the increase in the existence and use of social media platforms means that young people now have the ability to express themselves and shape the sharing and representation of their identity in ways that are unprecedented (Tshidzumba, 2019; Lin et al, 2015). Research suggests that impression management is something that users consider when on social media, and many choose to represent their "ideal self," which is the representation of traits and attributes that a person would like to possess or believes someone else would like them to possess instead of their "actual self," or the representation of the traits or attributes that a person believes they possess (Higgins, 1987; Siibak, 2009).

As digital natives/iGen, adolescents tend to join social media networks for social reasons and use their visual self-presentation in strategic ways. This is a format that they have grown up seeing others use, and it seems natural for them to be a part of social media communities. They often choose to share images that represent their ideal self, based on their understanding of what they perceive as being important to others with high social standing either online or both online and offline, and an adolescent may choose to represent themselves in different ways depending on the online peer group that they are trying to connect with socially (Siibak, 2009). When using social media, people may work to extend their offline persona, but they may also choose to use the medium to create a new persona, reinventing themselves through the platform (Popescu, 2019). It's also important to know that social media can impact the social experiences of teens by offering new opportunities for compensatory behaviors that would be less likely in face to face interactions (Nesi, Choukas-Bradley & Prinstein, 2018). Research on the effects of computer mediated communication, which includes social media interactions, supports the concept of "online disinhibition effect (Suler, 2004). The online disinhibition effect means that specific features of the online environment, such as not receiving immediate feedback from peers due to the asynchronous nature of the communication and not being able to pick up on verbal or facial cues of the victim, create a setting in which people are more likely to do or say things that would not in a face to face context.

Remember, media is a tool. It can be used to build social connections and share oneself in constructive ways, and it can also be used to construct a representation of identity that may not be accurate. Since our students are approaching social media as digital natives/iGen, they may view its ubiquity in their lives as normal and expected. It is possible that as they were growing up they may have seen their own parents and other caregivers use social media extensively. As we approach the concept of choosing how to use social media intentionally, it is key to do so with empathy, understanding that questioning the use of social media may be a foreign concept for some of our students. It is our goal to help students identify their own reasons for using social media, consider how they want others to perceive them and think about how their use of these platforms contributes to their desired presentation or takes away from it.

References

Higgins, E. T. (1987). Self-discrepancy: A theory relating self and affect. *Psychological Review*, 94, 319-340.

Nesi, J., Choukas-Bradley, S., & Prinstein, M. J. (2018). Transformation of Adolescent Peer Relations in the Social Media Context: Part 2-Application to Peer Group Processes and Future Directions for Research. *Clinical Child & Family Psychology Review*, 21(3), 295–319. https://doi.org/10.1007/s10567-018-0262-9

Popescu, M. M. (2019). Personal Online Identity-Branding or Impression Management. **Buletin Stiintific**, 24(1), 67–75. https://doi.org/10.2478/bsaft-2019-0008

Qiu, L., Lu, J., Yang, S., Qu, W., & Zhu, T. (2015). What does your selfie say about you? *Computers in Human Behavior*, 52, 443–449. https://doi.org/10.1016/j.chb.2015.06.032

Rideout, V., and Robb, M. B. (2019). *The Common Sense census: Media use by tweens and teens, 2019*. San Francisco, CA: Common Sense Media.

Rideout, V. & Robb, M.B. (2018). *Social media, social life: Teens reveal their experiences.* San Francisco, CA: Common Sense Media.

Siibak, A. (2009). Constructing the Self through the Photo selection - Visual Impression Management on Social Networking Websites. Cyberpsychology: *Journal of Psychosocial Research on Cyberspace*, 3(1), Article 1. Retrieved from https://cyberpsychology.eu/article/view/4218

Suler, J. (2004). The online disinhibition effect. *CyberPsychology & Behavior,* 7(3), 321–326. https://doi.org/10.1089/1094931041291295.

Tshidzumba, N. A. (2019). The Selfie Culture: Identity Creation and Status Conferral on Social Media. *Gender & Behaviour, 17*(3), 13577–13584. Retrieved from http://search.ebscohost.com/login.aspx?direct=true&AuthType=sso&db=a9h&AN=139753108&site=eds-live&scope=site

Twenge, J. M., Martin, G. N., & Spitzberg, B. H. (2019). Trends in US Adolescents' media use, 1976–2016: The rise of digital media, the decline of TV, and the (near) demise of print. *Psychology of Popular Media Culture*, 8(4), 329–345. https://doi.org/10.1037/ppm0000203

Twenge, J. M. (2017). Have smartphones destroyed a generation? *The Atlantic*, 20 (September 2017), https://www.theatlantic.com/magazine/archive/2017/09/has-the-smartphone-destroyed-a-generation/534198/.

Bloom's level of thinking: evaluation

Objective: In their study of interaction with media, students will explore connections between identity in real life and identity online.

Grouping: whole class and individual

Materials and resources: scrap paper, sentence strips, sticky tack or tape, computer/projector with featured video for discussion

Time: 30-45 minutes

Description of the learning process:

The teacher will:

1. Ask students to jot down on scratch paper words and phrases that they think describe themselves (AT THIS POINT, DO NOT REVEAL THE ACTIVITY OR TOPIC FOR THE DAY).

2. Ask them to jot down in a separate column, words or phrases that someone ELSE would use to describe them (they may be some of the same or some different).

3. After the students set the scratch paper aside, play the chosen video (the teacher will have selected a video from youtube with a person singing who presents themselves to be a good singer, but it is not good at all… check the worst American Idol singers, etc) .

4. Invite students to write in all caps on a sentence strip with unidentifiable handwriting a comment that they might leave under that video if it were posted on social media or the internet. Ask them to be clever, witty, and winsome! These comments need to be written where no one else can see them! No names!! Then students will "turn in" their comment on a designated table/desk upside down.

5. Mix up the comment strips and ask students to come pick one up (not their own) and place it on the white board with sticky tack (or tape).

6. Ask students to now go write their names on the sentence strip they wrote. THEN PAUSE. If students hesitate, ask them if they'd like another shot at writing a comment and offer another sentence strip. This would be appropriate if they'd

been a bit degrading or judgmental or rude in their initial comment and realized they'd rather not have their name attached to that comment.

7. Whether or not they chose to rewrite the comment… ask them if the comment they wrote lines up with how they described themselves at the beginning and how they hope others would describe them.

8. As time permits, discuss with them the ways in which our online identity needs to line up with our real identity, online disinhibition, and its dangers.

The student will:

1. Jot down on scratch paper words and phrases that you think describe yourself.

2. Jot down in a separate column, words or phrases that someone ELSE would use to describe you (they may be some of the same or some different).

3. View the video chosen by your teacher.

4. Write in all caps on a sentence strip with unidentifiable handwriting a comment that you might leave under that video if it were posted on social media or the internet. Be clever, witty, and winsome! These comments need to be written where no one else can see them! No names!! Turn in your comment upside down.

5. Pick up one comment that is not your own and place it on the white board with sticky tack (or tape).

6. Write your name on the sentence strip you wrote.

7. Ask yourself the following question: Does the comment you wrote line up with the ways you described yourself at the beginning of this activity or the ways you hope someone else would describe you?

Extension:
Bloom's level of thinking: evaluation

Grouping: large group

Materials: statements for consideration

Time: 30-45 minutes

Expanding on #8 above, the students will consider reasons and motivations behind online disinhibition. As a group, create a working definition of disinhibition. The teacher then designates one wall of the room as "strongly agree" and the opposite wall as "strongly disagree." Explain that the imaginary line between the two walls represents a continuum between the two polarities. Use any of the following questions and instruct students to stand on the imaginary line where they see themselves to be.

1. When having a conversation with someone face to face my response is often based on their reaction.

2. When having a conversation with someone face to face I wait for the other person to complete their sentence before responding.

3. When having a conversation with someone face to face I often say something that risks my physical or emotional safety.

4. When engaging with someone online I spend a long time thinking about how I will respond before typing.

5. When engaging with someone online I picture the other person's reaction as I reply.

6. When engaging with someone online I often say something that would risk my physical safety if I were face to face with the person.

7. When engaging with someone online I often say something that calls into question the other person's character.

After each statement is read and students move to their chosen spot on the "line," invite students to voice their thinking about where they've chosen to stand. Return to the conversation about disinhibition and ask students why people may feel less inhibition online than in real life. Discuss what this means about one's identity if a person's online presence is very different from how they interact face to face. Invite students to create a personal statement about how they will interact online that matches who they want to be in real life.

Implicit Bias

Session three: In this session we will think about perspective and how it shapes how we see the world around us. We will also explore the ways our implicit or unconscious biases shape our perspectives. The activity for this session challenges students to consider how perspective and bias can completely change the way someone or something is perceived. The extension material moves deeper into implicit bias in order to make students more aware of their own unconscious biases they may hold.

SEL Core Competency: Self-awareness

Differences come in many forms, as can commonalities, and we can belong to many different kinship groups. Kinship groups are groups of people that have something in common (Banaji & Greenwald, 2013). As we grow up, all of us begin to learn how to tell who is a part of our kinship groups and who isn't. This social understanding helps us build connection, but it can also cause us to feel disconnected and unable to relate to or have empathy for those who we perceive as different from ourselves. Noticing differences isn't bias, it's the automatic assumptions that we make about people due to those differences that are connected to bias.

As we learn how to relate to others who are similar to or different from us, we develop implicit or unconscious biases. These are automatic associations we make about specific groups of people that affect the way that we respond to them. We may even be unaware of holding these beliefs, because these biases are deeply ingrained in our ways of understanding the world (Applebaum, 2019). Our biases may be positive or negative, and can focus around gender, race, weight, height, skin tone or any other aspect of a person's identity. Every person has implicit biases, or blind spots, that are outside of our awareness yet cause us to attribute characteristics to particular groups of people (Banaji & Greenwald, 2013). Digital natives/iGen students may find that they form categories of in and out groups based on social media interactions. Those who use social media and digital technologies frequently will likely be more likely to do so than their peers who are less digitally engaged.

Such blind spots can get in the way of our ability to authentically engage with others who are different from us, and can contribute to underrepresented groups feeling like they don't belong. They also make it difficult not only to empathize with people who we think are different from ourselves, but hinder our ability to work well with others and to learn and grow from interactions with those around us. The good news is, once we can identify our blind spots and know how they alter our perceptions, then we can learn to change our behavior and connect with folks from many different backgrounds (Banaji & Greenwald, 2013).

References

Applebaum, B. (2019). Remediating campus climate: Implicit bias training is not enough. *Studies in Philosophy and Education, 38,* 129-141. https://doi.org/10.1007/s!!217-018-9644-1.

Banaji, M. R., & Greenwald, A. G. (2013). *Blindspot : hidden biases of good people.* Delacorte Press.

Bloom's level of thinking: analysis

Objective: In their study of consequences of perspectives in media, students will consider the reality of subconscious bias based on perspective.

Grouping: individual, whole group

Materials and resources: strips of paper with instructions, pencils, plain white paper one sheet per student

Time: 30-45 minutes

Description of the learning process:

The teacher will:

1. Hand out paper, strips of paper with instructions, and pencils to students.

2. Without telling the students, divide up the large group into four groups. Each of the students in the smaller groups will have the same instruction strip. Students should not see each other's papers or know that there are different captions at the top of the page. Instruct students to silently draw with their pencil the picture that fits their instruction strip.

    The four groups are:

    ○ Draw a frog from the perspective of a fly
    ○ Draw a frog from the perspective of a fish
    ○ Draw a frog from the perspective of a 7 year old child
    ○ Draw a frog from the perspective of a biology student

3. After five minutes, without speaking, ask students to hold up their drawing and walk around to find the other students who have the "same" picture. Ask how they "found" each other and why the other drawings weren't like their drawing even though EVERYONE was drawing a frog.

4. Lead discussion about how media gives a skewed view and emphasizes certain things and neglects others. Ask what the various frog views emphasized and what they left out. Ask: Did you intentionally leave out important details? Discuss unintentional media bias based on perspective.

5. Offer a current story for the students to consider. Ask the students to explore the perspective of the various parties (family member of one murdered, the parents of the murderer, etc). Refer to the questions from Session 4 about who is the audience, what is left out, etc. if helpful.

6. Discuss why it might be important to realize there is unconscious bias in most media stories. Remind students that if the bias is unconscious, it lacks malicious intent, but still needs to be recognized when consuming media so we can be attentive readers and viewers.

The student will:

1. After receiving your instructions, draw what you were assigned by your teacher.

2. After five minutes, without speaking, hold up your drawing and walk around to find the other students who have the "same" picture. Discuss how you found your group.

3. Explore the perspective of the various parties in the story your teacher shares. Refer to the questions from Session 4 about who is the audience, what is left out, etc. if helpful.

4. Discuss why it might be important to realize there is unconscious bias in most media stories.

Extension:
Bloom's level of thinking: application, evaluation

Materials: Access to Harvard Implicit Bias website, playing cards, access to Aesop's Fables

Time: **Activity 1**: 15 minutes
        Activity 2: 15 minutes
        Activity 3: 15 minutes

Unconscious bias is difficult to comprehend for many children because of its abstract nature. The following extension activities will help create an initial framework in which students can begin to understand biases we might have without even knowing it.

1. Utilize the Harvard Implicit Bias website and their testing options. For middle school students, the initial card sorting activity is a clear introduction to our inability to sort quickly when the sorting does not fit the categories that seem most obvious to us.

2. The second activity is designed to alert students to the protagonists in their favorite books.

    ○ As a group, brainstorm the titles of the most popular fiction books for their class or grade.

    ○ After brainstorming, list the protagonist for each book beside the title. Discuss how many protagonists are white and how many are non-white. If the list seems inequitable, create a plan to develop a list of excellent YA fiction in which the protagonist is a person of color.

3. Ask students to recall Aesop's fable of the tortoise and the hare. Guide students in a discussion about what assumptions the hare made about the tortoise. How did those assumptions affect how the hare viewed the tortoise? What choices did the hare make based on those assumptions? Connect these assumptions to assumptions made in society about various groups of people (people in wheelchairs, people who are very short, people who haven't attended college, etc).

Bias and Worldview

Session four: In this session students will consider how various viewpoints shape the messages that are conveyed in media. They will learn how to spot bias in the media they consume. The Extension activity will introduce students to the concept of worldview and why it is important to consider when consuming media.

SEL Core Competency: Social awareness

All of us have a distinctive worldview that colors the way we see and thus interpret the world around us. A worldview is simply the lens through which we view the world, the assumptions that we make about truth, value, and humanity. As we discussed in Session 3, biases can influence the way that we see the world and both understand and interact with those around us. Biases are also part of what shapes our worldview. That's important to keep in mind as we explore the concept of both our own worldview and those of the makers of the media that we consume.

The people who develop media and marketing campaigns have their own worldviews. Their perspective will influence the programs and products that they develop. On top of that, these campaigns are promoting consumption. The point behind them is to sell something, so of course they will work to make consumers feel that they need it, whether it is a beauty product or the latest electronic gadget. Whenever an author of a book, television show, advertisement or movie creates a piece of media, they are sharing their own worldview whether blatantly or subtly. For example, in recent Disney television shows, one sees a consistent dichotomy of smart, sassy girl compared to goofy, bumbling boy. These themes are reliable enough to be picked up on by the tweens and teens who consume this media. If students are consistently consuming media that perpetuates a specific worldview about where an individual's value lies or what kinds of interests or traits one is expected to have based on gender, race or some other point of identity, then they will begin to be impacted by that worldview. This is important because worldview shapes a student's understanding of who they are and what makes them valuable. Students who are digital natives and part of iGen have been found to tend to have some specific worldviews that teachers will want to be aware of. For example, they tend to be more aware of issues of safety than previous generations and to be less accepting of social inequalities (Twenge, 2017). Of course, some students may not demonstrate these perspectives, but it is something to consider when discussing worldview with students of this generation.

When children begin to understand that each piece of media or marketing that they consume has been crafted to promote a particular perspective, they can learn to identify that perspective and ask themselves how they feel about it. Do they agree or disagree with the worldview presented? Recognizing that worldview exists, identifying the worldview of the maker of the media one is consuming and comparing that worldview to one's own all lead to the development of critical media literacy skills that allow the student to become an active, critical consumer.

References

Renee R. Hobbs, *Digital and Media Literacy: Connecting Culture and Classroom* (Thousand Oaks, CA: Corwin Press, 2011).

Twenge, J. M. (2017). Have smartphones destroyed a generation? *The Atlantic*, 20 (September 2017), https://www.theatlantic.com/magazine/archive/2017/09/has-the-smartphone-destroyed-a-generation/534198/.

Bloom's level of thinking: evaluation

Objective: In their study of media bias, students will identify bias in media and objectively report on a current event without bias.

Grouping: whole class and partners OR small groups

Materials and resources: video clips for assessing bias, possibly internet access to search for stories, paper, writing utensils

Time: 1-2 hours

The teacher will:

1. Ask students to define bias. Continue discussion about what constitutes bias in media.

2. Show selected video clips. Two suggestions are "Don Cherry-- on women at hockey games" on YouTube and "FOX news host attacks Muslim scholar who wrote about Jesus (Reza Aslan)." The first one is about sports and second one is about religions. If unable to locate these exact clips, find a suitable substitute to demonstrate bias in reporting. After each clip, lead students in discussing what bias they might have noticed.

3. As a group, guide class in brainstorming as many current events as possible (consider all: news, sports, entertainment, etc). Once a list has been generated, lead discussion on various "sides" of these events and how these "sides" might create a biased reporting of the story. Example: the NBA finals as reported by one team's reporter or as reported by a local news source for the other team.

4. Continue discussion by posing the questions: Is bias always negative? Why is it important to recognize bias in the media and in ourselves? Do this in whatever format works for your group.

5. Based on the generated brainstorming list, assign students to work in partners or very small groups to create a story/report from a perspective of a completely unbiased reporter. Example: An unbiased story about current presidential candidates, or about a mainstream band losing one of its members, or about the NBA finals.

6. As time permits, allow groups to peer review each other's reports. The following questions can be used for peer review:

    ○ Does the story give more than one viewpoint?

    ○ Is there information that might be left out?

- Is it free of emotionally charged words/phrases or identifying a group mentality (working class, unwed mothers, teenage drivers, etc)?
- Did the story avoid extremes (worst/best, highest/lowest)?

7. Share final product and debrief about how difficult it can be to remain unbiased.

The student will:

1. Define bias and discuss what constitutes bias in media.

2. Watch selected video clips and look for bias.

3. Brainstorm as many current events as possible (consider all: news, sports, entertainment, etc). Once a list has been generated, discuss various "sides" of these events and how these "sides" might create a biased reporting of the story.

4. Consider the following questions: Is bias always negative? Why is it important to recognize bias in the media and in ourselves?

5. Based on the generated brainstorming list, work with a partner or small group to create a story/report from a perspective of a completely unbiased reporter.

6. As time permits, peer review each other's reports. The following questions can be used for peer review:

7. Does the story give more than one viewpoint?

8. Is there information that might be left out?

9. Is it free of emotionally charged words/phrases or identifying a group mentality (working class, unwed mothers, teenage drivers, etc)?

10. Did the story avoid extremes (worst/best, highest/lowest)?

11. Share final product and debrief about how difficult it can be to remain unbiased.

Extension:
Bloom's level of thinking: evaluation

Grouping: large group

Materials: paper, writing utensil

Time: 30 minutes

The concept of worldview is abstract and difficult even for adults, so to ask preteens and young teenagers to consider their own worldview is a tall order. That said, many gifted children have already wrestled with deeper ideas like worldview well before their age peers. This extension activity is definitely most suited to students who are willing and eager to think deeply about personal matters and will be able to be self-reflective.

Lead a brief conversation with the students defining worldview. A basic definition of worldview is how one looks at the world, how one thinks it operates, why things happen the way they do, and what one's purpose is. Students will then write about their own worldview for 5 minutes based on the group conversation. The goal of this 5 minutes is to keep writing. Tell the students that formatting, spelling, punctuation do not matter. Ask them not to edit themselves, but rather to write what comes to their minds. This generative writing will likely feel quite private to the students. Students should not feel compelled to share their writing.

Lead the students in thinking through the following questions. Again, this might need to be done with little conversation depending on the level of trust in the group.

- What media do you consume regularly that affirms your worldview?
- What media do you consume that represents a different worldview?
- Does the worldview that media portrays matter? Why or why not?
- Do the digital media messages you create (social media, videos, etc) reflect your worldview? Should they?

Stereotypes and Halo Effect

Session five: In this session, students will explore stereotypes based on cultural beauty standards. They will also consider gender stereotypes prevalent in advertising and marketing.

SEL Core Competency: Relationship skills

From a bioecological perspective, media acts as a force within the exosystem that shapes and defines an adolescent's idea of acceptable appearance and behavior. In order to interpret where he or she falls on the continuum of acceptability, the student will compare her or himself to social models presented as ideal. The mass media across its many forms has been identified as a particularly potent purveyor of ideal behavior and appearance (Bell & Dittmar, 2011), and adolescents are particularly vulnerable to using celebrities and media depictions as social models (Groesz, Levine & Murnen, 2002). People who identify more strongly with media characters and celebrities and who have already developed concerns about their own appearance are more likely to be impacted negatively by stereotyped media images (Bell & Dittmar, 2011; Want, 2009). Digital natives/iGen will likely use social media as a tool for social comparison as well.

The halo effect is a cognitive bias where the perception of one trait, or characteristic of a person or object, is influenced by information about another, often irrelevant trait (Forgas & Laham, 2009). For example, I may meet a tall man and think he is good at basketball. In this case, the man's tallness is leading me to assume that he is a good basketball player, even though I have no information about how or if he plays sports. An early adolescent may see popular characters on their favorite shows depicted as wearing certain clothing or engaging in risky behaviors, and assume that to be popular they must follow suit.

As children grow, they begin to understand stereotypes in a more complex way and may be able to be more aware of halo effects. For example, both halo effects and stereotypes are often linked to gender. By the time they are about seven, children expand their ideas of gender to include personality traits and academic achievement areas as well as physical characteristics. We know that adults tend to describe more desirable traits such as leadership skills, ambition, self-confidence, and independence as masculine and less desirable traits such as being emotional, needing approval, getting feelings hurt easily, and passivity as feminine traits (Powlishta, 2000). We see children beginning to think about traits as linked to gender as well.

In early elementary school, children even begin to think about certain academic subjects as masculine or feminine. For example, language and performing arts tend to be more strongly associated with females while mathematics and sciences are more strongly associated with males. Interestingly, stereotypes also impact the way that children rate their own abilities in an area. For example, a girl with high math ability is more likely to rate her abilities lower than a boy with the same math ability would (Bhanat & Jovanovic, 2005).

Television commercials for children overwhelmingly present gender stereotypes, with pastel colors, cooperation, and indoor play associated primarily with girls and competition and outdoor play associated with boys (Kahlenberg & Hein, 2010). Johnson and Young (2002) examined the themes of gendered voice and words present in children's television commercials. Clear gender patterns were found in the types of verbs that were used in commercials featuring the different genders. Action, competition and destruction words, such as break, flip, hit, smash, transform and construct, were used most often in advertisements that featured boys and boy-targeted products. Verbs that focused on limited activity, feelings, and nurturing, such as look, see, wait, cuddle, and caring, were used most often in advertisements that featured girls and girl-targeted products. Another pattern that was found involved the use of verbs of agency or control. These words were found more often in boy-oriented advertisements than girl-oriented advertisements, with a ratio of over 4:1. This study also examined the ways that boys and girls spoke in advertisements aimed at children. In advertisements that were oriented to both girls and boys, boys spoke more and girls often spoke only in response to the actions or statements of boys. When we consider the use of the word "power" and related words, 21% of boy oriented advertisements used the words "power" or "powerful," but in all of the girl-oriented advertisements, there was only one incident of the word "power" being used, and it was in the context of identifying the maker of a Barbie car (Power Wheels) (Johnson & Young, 2002). The authors conclude, "Toy makers and their advertisers either make no effort to associate or may consciously avoid associating girl-toys with power or their potential to transfer power to their users" (Johnson & Young, 2002). Even in educational software, you see over and over that boys are represented as aggressive, active, and competitive while girls are dependent and passive (Sheldon, 2004). When young people repeatedly see these gender stereotypes, they begin to believe them. For those digital native/iGen students who are deeply engaged digitally, stereotypes depicted on social media platforms may have an impact on their attitudes and behaviors (Twenge, 2017).

References

Bell, B., & Dittmar, H. (2011). Does Media Type Matter? The Role of Identification in Adolescent Girls' Media Consumption and the Impact of Different Thin-Ideal Media on Body Image. *Sex Roles*, 65(7–8), 478–490. https://doi.org/10.1007/s11199-011-9964-x

Bhanot, R. & Jovanovic, J. (2005). "Do Parents' Academic Gender Stereotypes Influence Whether They Intrude on their Children's Homework?" *Sex Roles* 52, no. 9-10, pp. 597-607.

Forgas, J. P., & Laham, S. (2009). Halo effects. In R. Baumeister, & K. D. Vohs (Eds.), *Encyclopedia of social psychology* (pp. 499 – 502). Thousand Oaks : Sage Publications.

Groesz, L.M., Levine, M.P. and Murnen, S.K. (2002). "The Effect of Experimental Presentation of Thin Media Images on Body Satisfaction: A Meta-analytic Review." *International Journal of Eating Disorders* 31, 1: 1-16.

Johnson, F.L. & Young, K. (2002). "Gendered Voices in Children's Television Advertising." *Critical Studies In Media Communication* 19, 4, pp. 461-477.

Kahlenberg, S. & Hein, M.. "Progression on Nickelodeon? Gender-Role Stereotypes in Toy Commercials." *Sex Roles* 62, no. 11/12 (2010): 830-847.

Powlishta, K. K. (2000), "The Effect of Target Age on the Activation of Gender Stereotypes." *Sex Roles* 42, no. 3/4: 271-282.

Sheldon, J.P. (2004). "Gender Stereotypes in Educational Software for Young Children." *Sex Roles* 51, no. 7/8, pg. 433-444.

Twenge, J. M. (2017). Have smartphones destroyed a generation? *The Atlantic*, 20 (September 2017), https://www.theatlantic.com/magazine/archive/2017/09/has-the-smartphone-destroyed-a-generation/534198/.

Want, S. C., (2009). "Meta-analytic Moderators of Experimental Exposure to Media Portrayals of Women on Female Appearance Satisfaction: Social Comparisons as Automatic Processes." *Body Image* 6, no. 4: 257-269.

Bloom's level of thinking: evaluation

Objective: In their study of stereotyping and halo effect in media, students will scrutinize the pitfalls of not recognizing and acknowledging stereotyping and halo effect.

Materials and resources: pictures for evaluating, dry erase markers, paper, writing utensils

Time: 30-45 minutes

Description of the learning process:

The teacher will:

1. Show students pictures on the screen of unknown people who have extreme physical characteristics (beautiful, ugly, harsh, overweight, etc).

2. Ask students to jot down their first thought about each person's character in each picture. Example: a picture of a beautiful woman might elicit a first thought that she looks nice.

3. Ask students to share (voluntarily!) why they assigned different character traits to different people.

4. Discuss halo effect and why it is detrimental and sets many people up for immediate failure and others up for success with no basis in reality.

5. Ask students how halo effect and stereotyping are alike and different. Discuss.

6. During this time, hang up pictures around the room and ask students to walk around to the different pictures writing what stereotypes they might notice in the various pictures/advertisements.

7. Split the class into boys and girls. If possible, one teacher joins the group of boys and one with the group of girls. Ask if they have ever felt stereotyped and if so, how does it feel? How might it feel to others? Come up with 3-4 steps/questions as a group to ask/consider in order to avoid falling into an automatic stereotype trap.

The student will:

1. Observe the images on the screen.

2. Jot down your first thought or impression about each person's character in each picture.

3. Share why you assigned the various character traits to different people.

4. Consider how halo effect and stereotyping are alike and different. Discuss with the class.

5. Look for stereotyping in the various pictures/advertisements your teacher shares.

6. In groups split by sex (boys in one group and girls in another) discuss if you have ever felt stereotyped and if so, how does it feel? How might it feel to others? Come up with 3-4 steps/questions as a group to ask/consider in order to avoid falling into an automatic stereotype trap.

Extension:
Bloom's level of thinking: application and analysis

Grouping: large group/individual

Materials: paper, writing utensils

Time: one hour

As a large group, lead a conversation about what traits culture assigns to little girls and which are assigned to little boys. Discuss how products are marketed to children based on those projected stereotypes. Topics for consideration might be books, bedroom decor, toys, and graphic t-shirts. As time permits, students could explore online shopping sites for these stereotypes. If possible, look at advertising from various retailers for examples. The students can make a list of their findings. Following the discussion, students will create an advertisement for a product that opposes cultural stereotypes. The advertisement will include words and images that break down gender stereotypes.

Permanence of Generating online content

Session six: In this session, students will consider ethical thinking with regard to how they interact with those they know in real life and online strangers. The activities will address one's online reputation and the permanence of content created in online spaces.

SEL Core Competency: Responsible decision making

Today's tween and teenagers, sometimes referred to as digital natives/iGen, have "grown up digital" (Tapscott, 1997,Prensky, 2001, Twenge, 2017), with their communication practices, ethics and identity shaped by their interactions with and use of digital media (James, 2014; Flores & James, 2012). From their comfort level in using digital media to share information to their knowledge of world events and popular culture, adolescents use digital media in many ways. According to recent research (Rideout & Robb, 2019), the average amount of time that teens spend on social media each day is just over an hour (1 hour 10 minutes). The frequency of use has increased over the past 5 years, with 63% of teens saying they use social media everyday compared to 45% in 2015. Forty one percent of teens reported enjoying social media "a lot." As teachers of middle school students, it's important to note that the median age that teens reported beginning to use social media is 14.

If the students in your classes aren't already using social media, they likely will begin to do so fairly soon. So, this is a great time to begin to help them to begin to think about the concept of digital reputation management. This means providing students with opportunities to think about how their behavior online might impact others and it's long-term impact on their own reputation. There are both benefits and challenges for tweens and teens navigating social media. There are opportunities to connect with new people and learn new things, but also the potential to harm others and themselves. That harm often manifests not from an intention to hurt others, but from what James (2014) says is "a failure to consider the potential effects of one's actions on other people, known and unknown (James, 2014,pg. 3). James (2014) calls these failures blindspots, and this session is designed to aid students in uncovering those blindspots, begin to consider and anticipate the potential effects of their own behavior on social media, and come to understand the permanence of digital artifacts and how those may impact themselves or others long term. James focuses on helping students develop ethical "ways of thinking" that consider the good of three groups, self, known others and others in a larger community.

In working with students to develop ethical thinking with these three groups in mind, James (2014) suggests three forms of thinking. The first form is thinking about roles and responsibilities, with a focus on developing awareness of the commitments that the student has in existing relationships (e.g. family, clubs, friendships). The second form is what James calls complex perspective taking, or learning to think about how one's own online behaviors might affect multiple different people, for example, their family members, friends or teachers. The third form of thinking is community thinking, considering the potential harms and benefits to larger groups, such as their school, city or other groups.

As students begin to develop these ways of thinking, they will become more effective digital citizens who are able to consider the effects of their use of digital media and develop an understanding of how to best manage their own online reputation.

References

James, C. (2014). *Disconnected : Youth, New Media, and the Ethics Gap.* The MIT Press.

Prensky, M. (2001a). Digital natives, digital immigrants part 1. On the Horizon, 9(5), 1–6. https://doi.org/10.1108/10748120110424816

Rideout, V., and Robb, M. B. (2019). The Common Sense census: Media use by tweens and teens, 2019. San Francisco, CA: Common Sense Media.

Tapscott, D. (1997). Growing up Digital. *Informationweek*, 655, 64.

Twenge, J. M. (2017). Have smartphones destroyed a generation? *The Atlantic*, 20 (September 2017), https://www.theatlantic.com/magazine/archive/2017/09/has-the-smartphone-destroyed-a-generation/534198/.

Bloom's level of thinking: analysis

Objective: In their study of consequences of media posting and permanence of online content, the students will draw conclusions about wise decision making when posting online.

Grouping: small groups, whole group, individual

Materials and resources: tubes of toothpaste, sentence strips, markers, paper towels, sticky tack, tape

Time: 30-45 minutes

Description of the learning process:

The teacher will:

1. Distribute paper towels and tube of toothpaste to groups of 3 students.

2. Ask students to squirt the tube of toothpaste onto the paper towel. Then ask them to get the toothpaste back in the tube. Clearly impossible.

3. Ask students to come up with a pretend twitter name for themselves that no one would recognize (and don't tell anyone!).

4. Show the students the tweet for the activity. The tweet is a picture of a teenager who has colored her hair green with the following text: "omg. I did it! I h8 u @ baseballkiller! U said green would luk bad but ha! I luk awesome!"

5. Ask students to write a response (280 characters) to the tweet on a sentence strip. Tell them to be clever, witty, and attempt to get lots of "likes."

6. Collect all responses in a pile and students pick up one that is not their own to hang up on the board using sticky tack or tape.

7. Ask students to move around the room making a checkmark on each comment they "like."

8. Randomly point out a comment and ask the students to describe this person based solely on an anonymous tweet. Ask them what that person is like.

9. Guide students in making the connection between this activity and online content they post. Ask students if they or someone they know has posted something that they wish they could take back and obviously cannot take back.

10. Show the video or written story about a woman (Justine Sacco) traveling to Africa having tweeted about AIDS and by the time she arrives in Africa, her twitter account has exploded and she has lost her job.

11. As time permits, spur discussion on how being anonymous sometimes gives us false security to say things we might not say in person or with our name attached. Tell them we will throw these away, but online, the comment is permanent...the toothpaste will not go back into the tube.

The student will:

1. With your group, squirt the tube of toothpaste onto the paper towel. Then try to put it back into the tube.

2. Create a pretend twitter name for yourself that no one would recognize (and don't tell anyone!).

3. View the tweet for this activity.

4. Write a response (280 characters) to the tweet on a sentence strip. Be clever, witty, and attempt to get lots of "likes."

5. After all the strips are submitted, randomly pick up one that is not your own and add it to the wall with sticky tack or tape.

6. Move around the room making a checkmark on each comment you "like."

7. Respond to the teacher's prompt about what various commenters are like as people.

8. Brainstorm stories of people posting something that they wish they could take back.

9. Watch the video of Justine Sacco.

10. Participate in the discussion with the class about online content permanence.

Extension:
Bloom's level of thinking: application and evaluation

Grouping: individual, large group, partners

Materials: paper, writing utensils

Time: 30-45 minutes

Ask students to consider their future goals for college and their professional life. Many students at this age will only have a vague notion of what they might want to do for college or for a profession, but most gifted students often know they want to go to a certain type of college and have dreams of a career even if it's not fully formed. Share with the students that in many college applications and applications for internships, letters of recommendation are needed. Ask students to think of an adult they trust who could write a letter of recommendation for them in the future. The students will then pretend to write the letter they hope that adult might write on their behalf. In other words, the student will write a letter that reflects how they hope a trusted adult will view them someday. After the students have completed the letters, lead the students in a discussion about how social media content might affect someone's ability to recommend a student for college, an internship, or a job. What kind of social media content might reflect poorly on a student's character? What types of social media content might show a student's positive traits? In partner groups, students will share their letters with each other and write down some personal guidelines for posting on social media based on how they hope others will view them.

Being an Active Consumer

Session seven: In this session students will consider the importance of being an active consumer of media rather than passively letting media come to them. The extension activity takes a deep look at the complicated topic of fake news and other misleading types of media.

SEL Core Competency: Responsible decision making

Throughout this workbook, we have built primarily on the bioecological model, with a focus on the interactions between the student as an active learner and her environment. The important thing to remember about this perspective is that rather than being a passive consumer of media, the student is powerful and active. The approach of teaching students to become critical consumers of media is vital. In this session we will share strategies to engage youth in the active examination of media that allows them to enjoy and learn from it, noting examples of both positive portrayals and ones that they perceive as more negative.

Teachers should remember that our digital natives/iGen students may bring specific digital literacy skills to their interactions with digital media that provide them with a unique perspective. Keep in mind that those students who have had less access to digital media may not share those points of view. Allowing students to openly talk through their own experiences with different types of media is helpful in providing you with understanding about the full range of thoughts that your students bring to the media literacy work that you are doing together.

Bronfenbrenner viewed the process of development as one in which the child can learn to fit into the existing environment and those expectations, but can also change the order of things through her own actions (Bronfenbrenner, 1979, 1992, 2005, Bronfenbrenner & Morris, 1998; 2006). When we provide children with the tools to critique and challenge the messages from media and marketing, they can become change makers. Their actions through media literacy programs, activism, and creation lead to change in their environment.

Whenever an author of a book, television show, or movie creates a piece of media, they are sharing their own worldview and values. We've already considered that if students are consistently consuming media that perpetuates a specific worldview or value, then they will likely begin to be impacted by that worldview. In this session, we want to support our students in learning how to develop their own worldview based on their individual and community beliefs and values and how to compare the worldviews presented through popular media to their own.

The way that children learn to engage with, interpret, and respond to media messages is mediated by interpersonal variables within their lives. The bioecological systems within a child's life, including his own unique characteristics as well as the microsystems of family, school and community and the macrosystem of larger culture provide a child with assets or challenges to effectively respond to media. With the help of caring adults, students can learn how to process and evaluate media messages on their own terms.

When adolescents begin to understand that each piece of media or marketing that they consume has been crafted to promote a particular perspective, they can learn to identify that perspective and ask themselves how they feel about it. Do they agree or disagree with the worldview presented? Promoting the idea of students as empowered consumers, activists, and creators is a strong stance that gives the student control, giving them the chance to identify their own power in making informed choices.

Adolescents themselves are great advocates for their perspective because they are at a particular stage of development when their power to resist peer pressure is growing (Pfeifer, Masten, Moore, Oswald, Mazziotta, Iacoboni & Dapretto, 2011). Many adolescents are hungry to make a difference in the world, to be world changers. By harnessing that energy and helping them to become critical media consumers, we can lend them a hand in learning to critically evaluate media and marketing campaigns. Using social media and word of mouth, adolescents and caring adults can work together to advocate for healthy behaviors and worldviews.

References

Bronfenbrenner, U. (1979). *The Ecology of Human Development* (Cambridge, MA: Harvard University Press, 1979)

Bronfenbrenner, U. (1992). *Six Theories of Child Development: Revised Formulations and Current Issues*, ed. Ross Vasta (London: Jessica Kingsley) 187-249.

Bronfenbrenner, U. (2005). *Making Human Beings Human* (Thousand Oaks, CA: Sage).

Bronfenbrenner, U. & Morris, P. A. (1998). "The Ecology of Developmental Processes," in Theoretical Models of Human Development, ed. Richard M. Lerner, vol. 1 of *Handbook of Child Psychology*, 5th ed., ed. William Damon (New York: Wiley, 1998), 993-1028;

Bronfenbrenner, U. & Morris, P. A. (2006). "The Bioecological Model of Human Development," in Theoretical Models of Human Development, ed. Richard M. Lerner, vol. 1 of *Handbook of Child Psychology*, 5th ed., ed. William Damon (New York: Wiley).

Jennifer H. Pfeifer, Carrie L. Masten, III, William E. Moore, Tasha M. Oswald, John C. Mazziotta, Marco Iacoboni, and Mirella Dapretto. "Entering Adolescence: Resistance to Peer Influence, Risky Behavior, and Neural Changes in Emotion Reactivity." *Neuron* 69 (2011): 1029-1036.

Bloom's level of thinking: evaluation

Objective: In their study of media consumption, students will judge the purpose, intent, audience, and values of various media messages.

Grouping: whole group, small groups

Materials and resources: internet access, Dove commercial

Time: 1 to 1½ hours

Description of the learning process:

The teacher will:

1. Ask students what questions they ask themselves when watching TV shows, videos, movies, commercials, etc. Likely they don't ask any!

2. Remind the students of the effects of media consumption and ask for reactions.
   - Can be addictive
   - Makes us compare our lives with others
   - Makes us restless
   - Gives rise to cyberbullying
   - Glamorizes risky behavior
   - Can make us dissatisfied
   - Can make us feel left out

3. Introduce the five questions by Renee Hobbs that can be asked to be a more active media consumer rather than passive.
   - Who is the creator of the piece and what is its purpose?
   - How does the creator of the piece attract and hold your attention?
   - What lifestyles, values, and worldviews are represented?
   - How might different people interpret this message?
   - What is left out?

4. Using Hobbs' questions, curate a list of clips from students' favorite shows, movies, videos. Include advertisements for products they like. Students could help generate these clips and advertisements. View the various clips or images.

5. Asking these questions makes us active consumers of media, not passive consumers. Discuss with them what happens when we passively consume media. We often see something that is NOT there or don't see something clearly. As an example, show Dove's commercial from YouTube titled "Dove Evolution" in which a one minute video shows how a regular woman is altered using make-up, hair changes, and then digital enhancements.

6. As time permits, challenge students to consider ways they can be more of an active consumer of the media they choose on a daily basis.

The student will:

1. Brainstorm what questions you ask yourself when watching TV shows, videos, movies, commercials, etc.

2. Consider your teacher's reminders on the effects of media consumption.

3. Consider the following questions by Renee Hobbs as you view various clips that your teacher has compiled.

    ○ Who is the creator of the piece and what is its purpose?
    ○ How does the creator of the piece attract and hold your attention?
    ○ What lifestyles, values, and worldviews are represented?
    ○ How might different people interpret this message?
    ○ What is left out?

4. Asking these questions makes us active consumers of media, not passive consumers. Discuss with your classmates what happens when we passively consume media.

5. View Dove's commercial from YouTube titled "Dove Evolution."

6. Brainstorm ways you can be more of an active consumer of the media you choose on a daily basis.

Extension:
Bloom's level of thinking: evaluation

Grouping: small groups, whole class

Materials: internet access, computer, paper, writing utensils

Time: 1 to 1½ hours

An increasingly important part of being an active consumer of media is recognizing fake news. A student's view of the concept of fake news will vary depending on their parents/caregivers' perspective on news sources, bias, politics, and level of trust of media in general. The following activities provide ways to spot fake news.

Many students might believe that fake news is any news that paints a public figure or public situation they like in a poor light. Fake news by definition is junk news, pseudo-news, hoax news, alternative facts, or deliberate misinformation.

Begin by asking students if they believe they can spot fake news or fake information online easily. Show the following websites to students and lead a discussion about which of these might be real and which might be fake.

○ Website about best hunting dogs by the American Kennel Club

○ http://www.dhmo.org/: This website is a fake site created to show students how easy it is to look "real" and be fake.

○ The US Government site about how Senators are elected: https://www.senate.gov/artandhistory/history/common/briefing/Direct_Election_Senators.htm

In groups of 3-4 (depending on the size of the group), use a jigsaw method to look up some relevant terms. Assign each group one of the following terms to define and provide an example: clickbait, propaganda, satire/parody, misleading headlines, biased/slanted news. An extra topic would be sloppy journalism, but it is harder to define quickly and more challenging to find quick examples. Then jigsaw the groups so each new group has a person who looked up each of the different topics. The members of the new group will share about what they learned. By the end of this exercise, the entire group will be knowledgeable about all of the terms.

After the students have a better understanding of the relevant terms/topics, introduce them to the simple acronym for checking to see if a source is worth considering. The acronym is CRAAP.

- **Currency**: is the information current
- **Relevancy**: is the information relevant for your particular need
- **Authority**: does the author of the information have the authority or expertise to write on the topic
- **Accuracy**: is the information reliable, truthful, or correct based on evidence or peer review and is the information free from technical errors like spelling, grammar, punctuation
- **Purpose**: what is the reason this information exists in this location

There are multiple checklists online that students can use to move through the CRAAP Test if this is helpful. Knowing how to do this will benefit them throughout their school career as they conduct research, too.

Kahoot has a fun online quiz to see if students can recognize fake news here: https://create.kahoot.it/share/64c69e92-f024-443e-aefc-539dfd1226b4

Introduce students to fact-checking websites. There are several to choose from. At the writing of this book, some of the options are politifact.com, factcheck.org, and snopes.com.

Using what they've now learned, revisit the three websites above and think about how they would now see them with their new ability to evaluate online content.

Celebrity Culture

Session eight: This session will focus on how celebrities in the media influence our values and personal lifestyle beliefs. Celebrities often hold great influence and power over those who follow them closely. Their words and actions are often magnified and elevated as having greater importance than someone who is not famous or well-known. The activities in this session will guide students to remember that celebrity is often fleeting and is not the most stable footing on which to place one's values. The activities guide students to consider why a particular person is famous. They also help students evaluate whether or not the values they hold personally align with the values presented by the celebrity.

SEL Core Competency: Responsible decision making

In this session we will explore the myriad of ways that celebrities influence children and adolescents through various media. Children and adolescents are in the process of constructing their identity, and media is one of the forces in their lives that they use to help them figure out who they are, who they want to be, and who they think they should be. Adolescents are active media users. They do not simply soak up media content, but instead make sense of it from their own individual perspective and experience. For many adolescents, celebrities serve as social role models. This idea is linked with social comparison theory, in which people compare themselves to others and strive to achieve social rewards, like attention and popularity, by copying those who have achieved higher social status. You may find that your digital native/iGen students tend to use social media influencers as high status models as well. They may watch these influencers on YouTube, Instagram, TikTok or other social media platforms and find themselves attempting to imitate them.

Adolescents use celebrities as social models to which they compare themselves. In fact, Giles (2004) claims that one of the most important psychological influences of media for adolescents is the forming of what he calls "parasocial" relationships with celebrities.

As adolescents are forming their own identity, their use of celebrities as comparison figures leads them to look to the celebrity for guidance on values, attitudes, and behaviors, including negative behaviors (Giles & Maltby, 2004; North, Sheridan, Maltby, & Gillett, 2007). Involvement with celebrities in general has been shown to influence adolescents in their purchasing behavior, attitudes, and behavioral choices (Chia & Poo, 2009). As we help our students consider celebrity culture, we will give them the opportunity to think about the concept of fame and celebrity itself as well their own response to it.

Resources

Giles, D. C., & Maltby, J. j. (2004). The role of media figures in adolescent development: Relations between autonomy, attachment, and interest in celebrities. Personality & Individual Differences, 36(4), 813. doi:10.1016/S0191-8869(03)00154-5

North, A. C., Sheridan, L., Maltby, J., & Gillett, R. (2007). Attributional style, self-esteem, and celebrity worship. Media Psychology, 9(2), 291-308. doi:10.1080/15213260701285975

Chia, S. C., & Yip Ling, P. (2009). Media, celebrities, and fans: An examination of adolescents' media usage and involvement with entertainment celebrities. Journalism & Mass Communication Quarterly, 86(1), 23-44.

Bloom's level of thinking: Evaluation

Objective: In their study of celebrity culture, students will analyze the lives of celebrities and judge why their lives create meaning/value for culture.

Grouping: whole group

Materials and resources: strips of paper each with the name of a current celebrity, blank strips of paper, writing utensils

Time: 30-45 minutes

Description of the learning process:

The teacher will:

1. Move through a PowerPoint of celebrities from 20, 30, 40 years ago asking students if they know who past celebrities are. These could be some from the teacher's childhood!

2. Discuss the definition of celebrity and where these celebrities (from item one) are now.

3. Ask students to write 2-3 CURRENT celebrities (sports, entertainment, etc) on the blank strips of paper.

4. Students will add the new strips to the pile of celebrity names already generated by the teacher. Gauge the number of celebrity strips needed based on the size of the class. For a group of 20 students, each student can write down 1-2 celebrities and that would be plenty, but if the group of students is small, the teacher might need to add some celebrities to the mix.

5. Explain "Who Am I?" Game: Class is divided into two teams. A representative from each team stands in the front of the room. One representative blindly chooses a celebrity name from the pile. Each representative looks at the celebrity name, but doesn't tell anyone else. The representatives take turns giving one word hints to their teams to help them try to guess the celebrity first. The first team to guess the celebrity correctly receives a point.

6. Lead students in playing "Who Am I?"

7. Begin discussion about fame. What is it? The "has beens" we don't really remember even though they were famous. The current celebrities we mostly described in superficial ways based on the one word descriptions. Is fame something to strive for?

8. Continue discussion about the values and lifestyles that celebrities represent. Lead students to consider if these values and lifestyles reflect their own goals and values for their lives.

The student will:

1. Attempt to identify the celebrities on the slide presentation.

2. Define celebrity and identify where these celebrities (from item one) are now.

3. Write 2-3 CURRENT celebrities (sports, entertainment, etc) on the blank strips of paper.

4. Add the new strips to the pile of celebrity names already generated by the teacher.

5. Listen to the explanation of the "Who Am I?" Game: Class is divided into two teams. A representative from each team stands in the front of the room. One representative blindly chooses a celebrity name from the pile. Each representative looks at the celebrity name, but doesn't tell anyone else. The representatives take turns giving one word hints to their teams to help them try to guess the celebrity first. The first team to guess the celebrity correctly receives a point.

6. Play "Who Am I?"

7. Discuss fame. What is it? Is fame something to strive for? What values and lifestyles do these celebrities represent? Are these values and lifestyles reflected in your own goals and values?

Extension:
Bloom's level of thinking: evaluation

Grouping: individual

Materials: digital device(s) and journal

Time: **Day one**: 20 minutes
One week of journaling
Follow-up day: 30 minutes

Students have now considered celebrity culture and their own values and lifestyle goals. The students will now keep a journal of media interaction as self-reflection to check if their stated values and lifestyle goals align with their media interaction. The instructor should be comfortable with a wide variation in the students' values and lifestyle goals. The purpose of this extension is not to offer moral lessons, but rather to allow students to self-reflect.

Before beginning the journaling exercise, the instructor will guide students to identify their own personal values and lifestyle goals including, but not limited to: fairness, justice, religious beliefs, inclusiveness, being a good friend, following rules, being a good student, how you spend your time.

For a one week time period (or longer if the instructor deems necessary), students will answer the following items in a journal at the end of each day:

- How many minutes did I engage with media of any kind today?
- List 1-3 things you saw or heard today in any of the media you engaged that affirmed your personal values or lifestyle goals.
- List 1-3 things you saw or heard today in any of the media you engaged that opposed your personal values or lifestyle goals.

At the end of the week (or more), guide the students in reflecting on how their media choices align with their personal values or beliefs. If their media choices do not reflect their values, students can partner with another student to create goals of how they could adjust their media interaction to better align with their values.

Data Literacy: What is Big Data and why is it important for us to understand?

Session nine: This session will introduce students to the abstract concept that their internet searches are providing personal data for various companies and groups.

SEL Core Competency: Social awareness and Responsible decision making

Everytime we get online, we are generating data that can and is used to understand us and our behaviors. Whether it's what we buy or search for online to whose images and posts we like on social media, data is being collected and organized. Everytime we sign up to receive discounts or information, we're sharing our own data with companies that are putting it together to keep track of who we are in terms of age, gender, and geographical location, and what we are interested in purchasing or learning about. This information is called Big Data. As Grassegger and Krogerus (2017) explain, Big Data means that everything we do on and offline creates digital traces. All of that information is stored and can be used by those who want to sell us something and those who want to manipulate our behavior.

As we share our phone numbers, email addresses and names, third party data brokers are working across platforms to connect the dots between all of our different online activities and both our online and offline interests (Fontichiaro, 2019). Many people, both students and adults, don't understand that their online activity is being monitored and collected as data in order to develop a full digital picture of them as an individual. It is especially important to build this kind of digital literacy with digital native/iGen students, as their frequent exposure to life on and through the internet may make them less mindful about sharing their personal information online.

Students may think it's no big deal if their data is gathered for advertisements. After all, maybe it's a good thing for companies to know what they're looking to buy. Maybe that information leads them to bigger discounts. But it's important for all of us to understand that data isn't just gathered to sell us things, but to manage and manipulate our behavior in both big and small ways. For example, in 2016 a total of 87 million Facebook users, most of them in the United States, completed a quiz called "thisisyourdigitallife" that allowed Cambridge Analytica to gather information about them (Confessore, 2018). Cambridge Analytica then used this information to identify gullible voters in both the United States and the United Kingdom and created targeted misleading political advertisements to those voters in order to manipulate them to vote for the candidates who had hired them (Confessore, 2018; Grasseger & Krogerus, 2017). Many believe that both the 2016 U.S. election and the Brexit referendum in the United Kingdom were heavily influenced by the use of Big Data to target voters.

Digital data can also be used to monitor our behavior, and that may have big repercussions in our lives. For example, in August 2019 seventeen year old Ismail B. Ajjawi was all set to begin as a first year student at Harvard. However, when he landed in Boston, Custom and Border Protection agents searched his computer and smartphone and found what they deemed anti-American social media posts from connections of his. Ismail's visa was then cancelled and he was denied entry into the United State (Zraick & Zaveri, 2019). People have also gotten fired from their jobs for offensive posts on social media. A 2015 Rolling Stone magazine article shared seventeen stories of people who had lost their jobs over social media posts, with posts ranging from British bankers recreating an ISIS beheading to a hospital employee who advocated the indiscriminate shooting of crowds of protestors calling for racial equality (Halper, 2015). College students have had their offers of admissions rescinded from both private and public colleges and universities due to racists posts on social media. Some students were penalized for posts that had been created a year or two before their admissions into the institution (Levin, 2020).

All of these incidents make it clear why it is so important for students to build data literacy in order to understand how their online activity generates Big Data and how that data can be used.

References

Confessore, N. (2018, April 4). Cambridge Analytica and Facebook: The scandal and the fallout so far. Retrieved August 3, 2020 from https://www.nytimes.com/2018/04/04/us/politics/cambridge-analytica-scandal-fallout.html.

Fontichiaro, K. (2019). Data Literacy: Negotiating Convenience and Data Privacy. *Teacher Librarian*, 47(1), 51–54.

Grassegger, H. & Krogerus, M. (2017, January 28). The data that turned the world upside down. *Vice*. Retrieved August 4, 2020 from https://www.vice.com/en_us/article/mg9vvn/how-our-likes-helped-trump-win.

Halper, K. (2015, July 13). A brief history of people getting fired for social media stupidity. Retrieved August 4, 2020 from https://www.rollingstone.com/culture/culture-lists/a-brief-history-of-people-getting-fired-for-social-media-stupidity-73456/the-bankers-who-think-isis-killings-are-a-hoot-153345.

Levin, D. (2020, July 2). Colleges Rescinding Admissions Offers as Racist Social Media Posts Emerge. Retrieved August 2, 2020 from https://www.nytimes.com/2020/07/02/us/racism-social-media-college-admissions.html.

Zraick, K. & Zaveri, M. (2019, August 27). Harvard students says he was barred from U.S. over his friends' social media posts. *New York Times*. Retrieved August 3, 2020 from https://www.nytimes.com/2019/08/27/us/harvard-student-ismail-ajjawi.html.

Creating and Consuming Media Messages with Purpose: A Guide for Educators

Bloom's level of thinking: synthesis, evaluation

Objective: In their study of big data, students will identify ways in which big tech collects data on consumers and how their digital footprint is their technological trail.

Grouping: whole class and individuals

Materials and resources: paper, writing utensils

Time: 30-45 minutes

The teacher will:

1. Divide the students up into groups of 3-4 students per group.

2. Provide each group with one of the three profiles of middle school students at the end of this lesson.

3. Ask each group to pretend that they're trying to market to that student described in their profile. They will brainstorm some ideas of companies who might advertise to this person, groups for which that person might be interested, and other organizations of interest.

4. Guide the students in a conversation about how these various companies, groups, and organizations might market to each of the students in the profiles. Consider some of the following questions:

    1. Is this negative? Positive? Both? How?

    2. Why is it important to understand how people are targeted through one's online footprint?

    3. If a platform or online tool is free to use, how are they making money? How is advertising used? Is it overt on the platform? Or is your collected data sold to advertisers?

    4. Could stored personal data be used for nefarious purposes?

    5. How can a person's awareness of a digital footprint help make one more intentional about their own media production and consumption?

The student will:

In your assigned group, brainstorm ideas of companies who might advertise to the student described in your profile. Also brainstorm groups for which that person might be interested and other organizations of interest.

Discuss how these various companies, groups, and organizations might market to each of the students in the profiles. Consider some of the following questions:

1. Is this negative? Positive? Both? How?

2. Why is it important to understand how people are targeted through one's online footprint?

3. If a platform or online tool is free to use, how are they making money? How is advertising used? Is it overt on the platform? Or is your collected data sold to advertisers?

4. Could stored personal data be used for nefarious purposes?

5. How can a person's awareness of a digital footprint help make one more intentional about their own media production and consumption?

Extension:
Bloom's level of thinking: evaluation

Grouping: individual

Materials: questionnaire, paper, writing utensils

Time: one hour

Now that students have considered the mostly hidden concept of stored personal data and how it is used, they will have the opportunity to think like a company or group wanting to target an individual based on that individual's likes and preferences.

Students will fill out the form at the end of this session with their personal information. The teacher will then collect the forms from the students and then distribute them back out to the students so each student has a form of someone else in the class.

Based on the answers on the student information form, each student will create a plan to market and attract the attention of the student whose form they've been assigned. Encourage students to think broadly and creatively. They can write a narrative. They can include drawings or images that might be used to market to their assigned person. The following questions might be helpful:

- What companies would this person purchase from?
- What businesses could easily overly advertise to this person?
- What groups or organizations would capture this person's attention?
- How could someone market to this person in subtle ways that they might not notice?
- Are there any groups that might seek to do harm that could capture this person's attention?

After the students have completed this activity, allow them to share with the person they were working on and lead the class in a conversation about how they felt after seeing how their classmate targeted them.

Student 1 profile:
Mikayla is a 6th grader. She loves sketching, fiction books about pioneer days, and plays the piano. She has 3 sisters. Her family lives in a very small, rural town. She has a dog and a cat. She goes to a small school with about 40 students in her 6th grade class at a public school. Mikayla has not traveled outside of her city except to visit her grandparents who live an hour away from her house. Her parents are protective of what she watches, so she is only allowed to watch TV shows with her parents. Her time spent online is looking up drawing videos, music videos, and looking for new books to read. She shops at Walmart for clothes and goods. Her parents don't like to support big tech companies like Amazon. Mikayla browses Amazon to read book reviews. Mikayla's parents are fearful of their daughter being exposed to things online that could be dangerous, so they talk frequently about the harmful content that can be on the internet. Mikayla has never experienced anything scary online, so sometimes she secretly searches for some of the topics her parents warn her about to see if they are true. Mikayla isn't allowed to have any social media yet.

Student 2 profile:
James is in 8th grade. James spends hours a day playing online games. Many of the online games involve playing against other people who he doesn't know in real life. James has had a couple of these people message him privately with concerning questions, but he ignores them. James searches the internet for tips on how to play the online games better. He follows several youtubers who are gamers. James lives in a medium sized city and goes to a private school with little diversity. James' parents are both busy professionals, so they do not monitor his online time closely. He loves shoes and frequently searches online for the newest and best shoes. He aspires to learn how to play the drums so he can be in a band. He follows several drummers online. James loves his hometown's professional hockey team and follows their online presence closely. He also follows the sports teams for the college in his city. James is active on Twitter.

Student 3 profile:
Sierra is about to start high school. She lives in a huge, metropolitan area and her new high school has several thousand students. Sierra has a little brother and they live with their mom. Sierra's mom works the night shift at a hospital, so Sierra and her brother are often home in the evenings alone. They watch TV together and spend time online scrolling through social media and the internet. Sierra loves to follow Instagram influencers and celebrities. She is interested in lots of actresses and singers. She learns about different fashion designers from the celebrities she follows. She looks up make-up products she learns about. She enjoys watching make-up tutorials on youtube. Sierra is active on Instagram, Twitter, and Facebook.

Student personal information form

Name:

Age:

Favorite restaurants:

Favorite places to shop:

2-3 hobbies:

Favorite music:

Favorite brands (clothing, shoes, gadgets, etc):

Are you a gamer?

What social media platforms do you use?

What are 3 things you browse on youtube?

What are three things you browse on the internet in general?

What online shopping sites have you bought from?

What kinds of things have you signed up for online recently? Mailing lists? Business sites? Clubs? Any other places where you have entered personal information like name, address, city, phone number, birthday, age, gender, etc?

Media Creation

Session ten: In this final session that serves as a summative assessment, students will have the opportunity to synthesize all of the components of media consumption they have learned throughout these workbook activities.

SEL Core Competency: Responsible decision making

Having seen themselves as media critics, students can also learn to think of themselves as media makers. Teachers can help their student move from someone who passively accepts images and narratives presented by the media to someone who actively creates their own view, and then works to influence the views of those around them. Using high quality cameras on their laptop or smartphone, many students have ready access to the ability to record. Most adolescents are familiar with YouTube and other sharing sites and can use those to share their creations widely. Large media corporations are no longer the only ones who can widely disseminate their viewpoint. Now, students are capable of crafting their own stories and sharing their own worldviews widely. As they work to develop their own ideas and express their own values and belief systems, students will become even more aware of the techniques that media makers use to connect with and persuade their audience.

Although many digital natives/iGen students may have great familiarity with these tools and techniques, remember that the digital divide may have left some of your students without access to these tools. Be aware of those students who seem less comfortable and be prepared to help them learn how to use the tools and strategies that will empower them to become competent creators.

Media is influential. The beauty of artistic expression through various forms of media is that it can touch the audience right where they are. Our student media makers can learn to construct media from a perspective of social responsibility. Media makers work with mediums that move their audience, that persuade them, that make them believe, that make them laugh or cry. Media is a beautiful and powerful force. Students can learn to believe in the beauty that they can create and to think of the influence that they can wield through media making.

Using simple techniques and accessible tools, students can make potent statements promoting their own value systems. This provides an opportunity for positive activism. In this case, we use the term "positive" in reference to the fact that the media maker is adding something to the conversation. Rather than sitting back and being an armchair critic who feels powerless, beginning to think and act like a maker will give students the tools to view themselves as someone who has something important to share.

The key is that we have the tools to create media that we want to see and to comment critically and publicly upon products and programming that we do not like. Students can use these ideas to make a public statement promoting their own values or questioning those promoted by particular programs or products. If a student is really interested in producing quality media, they can try to get it produced professionally. Help them look for workshops, contests, and other opportunities to share the work as a media maker.

Bloom's level of thinking: evaluation

Objective: In their study of media creation, students will create a media message and a rubric/evaluation tool by which a person could evaluate a media message.

Grouping: whole class and smaller groups

Materials and resources: access to all of the content from the previous sessions in the workbook, writing utensils, paper, technology for creating media

Description of the learning process:

The teacher will:

1. Explain the concept of a free-range assignment. A free-range assignment is one in which students select their own method of expression to share their learning. The students will draw from their learning about the concepts and topics about media consumption in this workbook.

2. Provide a quick primer on the rhetorical proofs of ethos, pathos, and logos. You can spend as much or little time on this concept as you choose. The basic definitions students should know are:

   - Ethos: credibility, how credible the audience/reader perceives the writer or speaker to be
   - Pathos: emotional connection, how are feelings engaged
   - Logos: facts, logic

3. The students' task is to create a persuasive piece of media of their choice using ethos, pathos, and/or logos and considering the topics covered in this workbook.

   As a reminder, topics covered were:
   - Determining the target audience
   - Intent of the message
   - Online vs. in person identity
   - Perspectives a media message takes
   - Considerations of bias
   - Portrayal of stereotypes
   - The permanence of online content
   - Recognizing fake news
   - The sway of celebrity

The student will:

1. Listen to your teacher's explanation of a free-range assignment and the rhetorical proofs of ethos, pathos, and logos.

2. Create a persuasive piece of media of your choice using ethos, pathos, and/or logos and considering the topics covered in this workbook.

As a reminder, topics covered were:
- Determining the target audience
- Intent of the message
- Online vs. in person identity
- Perspectives a media message takes
- Considerations of bias
- Portrayal of stereotypes
- The permanence of online content
- Recognizing fake news
- The sway of celebrity

Extension:
Bloom's level of thinking: application and evaluation

Grouping: individual or small groups

Materials: paper, writing utensils, and/or rubric generator

Time: 1-2 hours

- Explain what a rubric is and its purpose. Show examples of rubrics/evaluation tools (checklists, etc) and how they might be used depending on the students' familiarity.

- Review all of the previous sessions completed in the workbook (in main activity in this session). If you have not done them all, the rubrics the students create will simply have fewer criteria.

- Lead students in discussion about creating a rubric/evaluation tool that would help someone evaluate media. As a group, determine the goal of the rubric in a simple sentence.

- Ask students to consider each of the topics or ideas one might consider when consuming media. Rubrics and checklists give structure to observation. What would one be "measuring" if applied to a rubric? What would one be trying to assess? What are the criteria for evaluating a media message (tweet, advertisement, video, etc)?

- In small groups, students will create their evaluation tool.

- When they are finished, each group will partner with another group for some informal peer evaluation. Encourage sharing of information and wording. There will likely be overlapping ideas since each group is working on the same task. Allow groups to edit as needed.

- Using media in previous sessions or the media students created in the main activity in this session, students will use their created evaluation tool as they consume the media messages. Allow students to then edit further as needed once they test out their creation.